Dear Charlotte,

Congratulations on your high school graduation! You are a very special young lady. May you be successful in whatever you pursue in your life. And may God's blessing and joy be with you always!

Love,
The Mak Family

PRESENTED TO:

_____

FROM:

_____

DATE:

_____

*Trust in the Lord with
all your heart and lean not
on your own understanding;
in all your ways acknowledge
him, and he will make
your paths straight.*

PROVERBS 3:5, 6

WHAT A WONDERFUL LIFE

for

GRADUATES

Standard
PUBLISHING
Bringing The Word to Life™

Published by Standard Publishing
Cincinnati, Ohio
A division of Standex International Corporation
Printed in China
© Copyright 2005 Mark Gilroy Communications, Inc.
6528 E. 101st Street, Suite 416
Tulsa, Oklahoma 74133
www.markgilroy.com

Designed and illustrated by jacksondesignco, LLC
Springdale, Arkansas
www.jacksondesignco.com

ISBN 0-7847-1800-8

Acknowledgments

Christy Philippe wrote "Praying Hands" on page 36-37, "In Just a Few Hours Work" on page 47, and "Where Is Your Calcutta?" on page 75.

Table of Contents

We can only be said to be alive in those moments when our **hearts** are conscious of our treasures.

THORNTON WILDER

Introduction

O ne of the most important tools for navigating your future is an attitude of gratitude.

How often do you stop to think about how wonderful your life really is? Are you savoring this exciting and challenging new time in your life?

No single attitude will change your outlook on life more profoundly and quickly than simple gratitude. Gratitude reminds you that even in the midst of challenges—big decisions, setbacks and difficulties, delayed goals—God's world is full of blessings and miracles. A thankful heart is a joyful heart.

As you read the following pages, let your heart and attitude be changed by a new sense of wonder that comes when you view life through the eyes of gratitude, optimism, and most importantly, faith in a loving God.

*God looked over
everything he had made;
it was so good, so very good!*

GENESIS 1:31 THE MESSAGE

Nature is the art
of God Eternal.

DANTE ALIGHIERI

WHAT A WONDERFUL WORLD

LIFE IS WONDERFUL BECAUSE HE PUT THE STARS IN THE SKY—AND HE CREATED AMAZING OPPORTUNITIES FOR YOU.

Take time
to **marvel**
at the
wonders
of life.

GARY W. FENCHUK

Your Brain

The human brain has about 15 billion cells. Of course, some people seem to use more of those cells than others!

One math genius of the 19th Century, Zerah Colburn, was asked how many seconds had elapsed since the birth of Jesus Christ. He answered correctly in five seconds. By the age of four, Kim Ung-Yong of Korea could speak Korean, English, Japanese, and German fluently. Gon Yang-ling of China has memorized more than 15,000 telephone numbers—yes, with names.

Even if you haven't accomplished mental feats like these, look how far you and your brain have come to reach graduation day! You truly have an amazing gift from an amazing God that makes life wonderful.

The more
I study
nature the
more I am
amazed at
the Creator.

LOUIS PASTEUR

God's Wild, Wonderful World

God's wonderful world is full of wild, wonderful animals with amazing gifts and talents. Did you know lizards can talk to each other? No, lizards don't make audible sounds the way other animals do. Instead, they convey their moods, intentions, and other messages through an astonishing display of athletic prowess: push-ups, elaborate head movements, body contortions, and the ever-popular swelling of the throat.

And have you ever wondered how those small lizards called geckos can walk up walls and across ceilings upside down? Scientists have discovered that a gecko's foot is covered with up to a million tiny hairs, each of which splits into as many as 1,000 tips.

The tips are so small that they interact with a surface on a molecular level. A tiny gecko of little more than an ounce, using all these tips at once, could support 280 pounds!

Remember: the one who made lizards able to communicate and walk on walls is the same one who created you with gifts and talents to make a difference in your world.

I love to think
of nature as
an unlimited
broadcasting
station, through
which God speaks
to us every hour,
if we will
only tune in.

GEORGE WASHINGTON CARVER

Counting Stars

Go outside on a clear night when the sky is filled with stars and gaze up into the heavens. Then hold out a dime at arm's length. If your eyes could see with the power of a telescope, you would have just blocked 15 million stars from your view!

Look up into the heavens. Who created all the stars? He brings them out one after another, calling each by its name. And he counts them to see that none are lost or have strayed away.

ISAIAH 40:26 NLT

To find the universal **elements** enough; to find the air and the water exhilarating; to be refreshed by a morning walk or an evening saunter; to be thrilled by the stars at night; to be elated over a bird's nest or a **wildflower** in spring—these are some of the rewards of the **simple life.**

JOHN BURROUGHS

To Do!

A Canoe Trip

When was the last time you really noticed and enjoyed God's world? To rekindle a sense of awe and wonder, plan a canoe trip or hiking excursion with some friends and fellow graduates. You may be too busy to go too far, but get as far away from the ordinary as you can on a day trip. While you're out in nature, take time to pray and worship and write songs to God. Thank him for old times and celebrate the future, all the while remembering that God is an awesome creator—and that he loves you!

It is a **glorious privilege** to live, to know, to act, to **listen**, to behold, to love. To look up at the **blue summer sky**; to see the sun sink slowly beyond the line of the horizon; to watch **the worlds come twinkling** into view, first **one by one**, and the myriads that no **man** can count, and lo! The universe is white with them; and **you and** I are here.

MARCO MORROW

Lord, you have created such a beautiful world. Just looking at a night sky, I'm amazed by the distance and beauty of the stars— the magnitude of your beautiful creation. Help me see your handiwork today, God. And help me remember that the one who created such a wide and wonderful world knows and loves me and will meet my every need.

For the Lord
delights in his people.

PSALM 149:4 NLT

Always be a
first-rate version
of yourself,
instead of
a second-rate
version of
somebody else.

JUDY GARLAND

What a Wonderful You

God made you unique and special.
Never forget how much you are loved.

The average person goes to his grave with his music still in him.

OLIVER WENDELL HOLMES

All My Songs Are Wonderful

Irving Berlin has been one of America's most-loved composers with more than one thousand songs in his catalog. Among many other familiar favorites, he wrote "I'm Dreaming of a White Christmas," the world's all-time best-selling musical score.

When Berlin was an old man in his 90s, an interviewer asked him: "Is there any question that you've never been asked, but would like to be?"

"Well, yes, there is one," he replied. "'What do you think of the many songs you've written that didn't become hits?' My reply would be that I still think they are wonderful."

God, too, has an unshakable delight in the things—and people—he has made. Whether or not they're a "hit" in the eyes of others, he thinks each of his children is wonderful!

As a bridegroom rejoices over his bride,
so will your God rejoice over you.

ISAIAH 62:5

25

Faith Is ...
Realizing that
I am useful to
God not in spite
of my **scars**
but because
of them.

PAMELA REEVE

YOU WERE BORN AN ORIGINAL; DON'T DIE A COPY!

Everyone is different, but sometimes those differences can make you feel insecure. It's tempting to fit in at any cost, but mindless conformity robs you of the joy of being uniquely you.

Instead of wasting your time comparing yourself to others and feeling envious, rejoice and give thanks for the wonder of who you are.

Celebrate the wonderful attributes God has given you. Dwell on the gifts you have instead of wishing for others. Revel in knowing that God knew you before you were even born and purposely made you as you. When was the last time you expressed your gratitude for such an amazing gift?

Accept yourself, but don't stop there. Practice viewing others in the same way: as unique, beloved creations of God.

WOW, YOU HAVE WONDERFUL HAIR!

God knows you inside and out. The Bible says that God knows you so well that he has even counted every hair under your mortarboard and tassel. Scientists say that there are approximately 100,000 hairs on the human head—give or take the 100 or so we lose each day. That's a lot of counting!

God cares so much for you that he wants to know everything about you. You are unique and special—because he created you that way! Never forget that every part of you—even the hairs on your head—are wonderful in his eyes.

We all have the
extraordinary
coded within
us, waiting to
be released.

JEAN HOUSTON

My Life So Far...

Write a letter to yourself as a reminder of how far you've come to reach graduation. Remember the hard times and obstacles and how they've made you stronger. Take stock of the qualities that lie within you that will help you in the future. And most of all, recall God's amazing love for you.

Tuck your letter in your Bible or in a notebook—anywhere you'll see it from time to time and be reminded that God cares for and values you.

We are ourselves, creations. And we, in turn, are meant to continue creativity by being creative.

JULIA CAMERON

*Thank you
for making me so
wonderfully complex!
Your workmanship is
marvelous—and how
well I know it.*

PSALM 139:14 NLT

Lord,

You made me with a purpose and you are pleased with your creation. I know that you have great plans for my life—plans to use my gifts and talents. Thank you for loving me so much that you bring my life meaning and shower me with your love.

Thank you so much for considering me to be your friend, and for fulfilling your plans for me. Help me today to live my life as one who is grateful to you.

*There are three things that
will endure—faith, hope, and love—
and the greatest of these is love.*

1 CORINTHIANS 13:13 NLT

Blessed are they who have the gift of making friends, for it is one of God's best gifts.

THOMAS HUGHES

WHAT A WONDERFUL FRIEND

YOUR LIFE BECOMES EVEN MORE WONDERFUL
AS YOU EXPRESS LOVE AND APPRECIATION
FOR THE PEOPLE IN YOUR LIFE.

Who, being loved, is poor?

OSCAR WILDE

Praying Hands

Two friends, Albrecht and Franz, both very poor, but both showing great promise as artists, made a deal. They would draw lots; the winner would continue in art school, while the other would work to support both of them. Once the winner finished school and began to make money as an artist, he would in turn support the other in his education and art career.

Albrecht won the drawing, finished his training, and went on to have a wildly successful career as an artist. And true to his word, Albrecht was ready to support Franz in his art studies. It was no longer possible, however, for Franz to be an artist. His fingers were now stiff and twisted from the manual labor. Amazingly, Franz did not succumb to bitterness—he was thrilled for his friend's success.

One day Albrecht found his friend kneeling, his misshapen hands intertwined in prayer. Struck by sudden inspiration, he grabbed his sketch pad and began work on what was to become his greatest masterpiece.

Five hundred years later, the works of Albrecht Durer can still be found in museums, galleries, and private collections. His paintings and sketches still appear in countless books. But none of his works are more famous and loved than "The Praying Hands" he sketched that day.

Greater love has no one than this,
that he lay down his life for his friends.

JOHN 15:13

Trees in the Storm

When a heavy snowstorm hit North Carolina, it was interesting to see the effect along Interstate 40.

Next to the highway stood several large groves of tall, young pine trees. The branches were bowed down with the heavy snow—so low that branches from one tree were often leaning against another.

Where trees stood alone, however, the effect of the heavy snow was different. The branches had become heavier, but without other trees to lean against, they snapped. They lay on the ground, dark and alone in the cold snow.

When the storms of life hit, God's wonderful world provides our example: Lean on your friends to see you through.

Carry each other's burdens, and in
this way you will fulfill the law of Christ.

GALATIANS 6:2

What do we live for if it
is not to make life less
difficult for each other?

GEORGE ELIOT

We are each of us angels with
only one wing, and we can fly
only by embracing one another.

LUCIANO DE CRESCENZO

If you have made another
person on this earth smile,
your life has been worthwhile.

SR. MARY CHRISTELLE MACALUSO

KISSING

Kissing—it's the ultimate expression of love, right? It may seem that way now, but in ancient Rome, kissing was a way of ranking a person's importance.

As a greeting, nobles of lofty status would kiss the emperor right on the lips. Ordinary citizens would only be able to kiss the emperor's hands. And servants were only allowed to kiss the least attractive body part of all—the emperor's feet!

There's a lot more to true love than just kissing. And learning to respect other people—no matter what their social status—is a good place to start. Love for other people, whether or not kissing is involved, is a wonderful thing!

Do not waste your time bothering whether you "love" your **neighbor**. Simply act as if you did. As soon as we do this, we find one of the **great secrets**. When you are behaving as if **you loved** someone, you will presently come to love him.

C.S. LEWIS

To Do!

The Friendliness Factor

You're heading for some major transitions, and are probably ready to make new friends. How are you doing on "friendliness"? Take a minute to evaluate yourself in the following areas:

- Listening
- Caring for others' needs
- Being ready to speak to new people
- Remembering names

What can you do to improve in these areas? You might ask a close friend, parent, or youth worker how you might need to improve your relationship skills, and for advice on how to go about it.

A friend is one of the nicest things you can have, and one of the best things you can be.

DOUGLAS PAGELS

43

POWERFUL AND DYNAMIC

Love can make mean hearts kind, turn enemies into friends, and heal even the most damaged of souls. But love is powerful only as long as it is active and persistent.

As you embark on this next stage of your life journey, be assured that your love will be challenged, but never forget—

- Love erases the effects of harsh words
- Love heals the heart that's been betrayed
- Love convicts the heart of those who are cruel
- Love brings clarity of purpose to times of misunderstanding
- Love builds bridges over chasms of mistrust
- Love protects a strong sense of self even in the face of mockery

No one has ever seen God; but if we love one another, God lives in us and his love is made complete in us.

1 JOHN 4:12

Father God,

*I thank you right now for your sons
and daughters who have—*

*Comforted me when I was hurting;
Provided support when I was weak;
Confronted me when I was spiritually drifting;
Given me confidence when I didn't believe in myself;
Offered me friendship when I was lonely;
Shown me truth when I was confused;
Prayed with me when I faced problems;
Counseled me when I needed direction.*

*I am so privileged to be a member of
your incredible household. I pray that you
would give me the strength today to love
the people in my life, and the wisdom to
see when people are hurting.*

*Please make me a person of kindness
and love as I go forward—help me
bring love to every life I touch.*

*Whatever your hand finds to do,
do it with all your might.*

ECCLESIASTES 9:10

Make no little plans.
They have no magic
to stir men's blood.
Make big plans: aim
high in hope and work.

DANIEL HUDSON BURNHAM

WHAT A WONDERFUL DAY

LIFE IS WONDERFUL—EVEN WHEN IT'S CHALLENGING!
YOU HAVE A LOT FACING YOU IN THE COMING DAYS, WEEKS,
AND YEARS, BUT WITH GOD'S HELP, YOU CAN FACE YOUR LIFE
WITH JOY AND A SENSE OF ACCOMPLISHMENT.

Go confidently in the direction of your dreams! Live the life you've imagined!

HENRY DAVID THOREAU

In Just a Few Hours Work

Is getting a high school degree really worth it? How about going on to college?

Henry Ford, the founder of Ford Motor Company, hired an electrical genius named Charlie Steinmetz to build the generators for a new factory. A few years later the generators stalled, and the repairmen couldn't find the problem. So Ford called Steinmetz, who tinkered with the machines for a few hours and then threw the switch. The generators whirred to life—but Ford got a bill for $10,000 from Steinmetz.

Flabbergasted, the rather tightfisted carmaker demanded to know why the bill was so high. Steinmetz wrote down: *For tinkering with the generators, $10; For knowing where to tinker, $9,990.*

Ford paid the bill. And whether or not you ever earn $10,000 in one sitting, you too will be rewarded when you passionately pursue wisdom.

> *The one who stays on the job has food on the table; the witless chase whims and fancies.*
>
> PROVERBS 12:11 THE MESSAGE

There are no great men in this world, only great challenges which ordinary men rise to meet.

WILLIAM FREDRICK HALSEY, JR.

Be Strong

Mielxto Saralegi of Spain hoisted a 721 pound stone onto his shoulders—about the same weight as five adults and, of course, a world record.

David Huxley of Australia pulled a Boeing 747-400, which weighs 197 tons, at the Sydney, Australia Airport.

Robert Galstyan of Armenia dragged two Russian railroad cars, weighing a total 215 tons, with his teeth.

Englishman Walter Cornelius pushed a bus more than half a mile with his head.

Another Brit, Mick Gooch, did sixteen pushups—using one finger balanced on a coconut.

As wonderful as those feats of strength are, the Apostle Paul encourages a different kind of strength—

Be strong in the Lord and in his mighty power. Put on the full armor of God so that you can take your stand against the devil's schemes. For our struggle is not against flesh and blood, but against the rulers, against the authorities, against the powers of this dark world and against the spiritual forces of evil in the heavenly realms. Therefore put on the full armor of God, so that when the day of evil comes, you may be able to stand your ground, and after you have done everything, to stand.

EPHESIANS 6:10-13

God,
give me hills to climb, and strength for the climbing!

ARTHUR GUITERMAN

Set Your Sights High

We rise to the level of the targets we set for ourselves.

Salesmen understand this principle. Studies show that if they set a goal for themselves, they usually reach it—but rarely exceed it. It happens in school all the time. When a student is just trying to get by in order to pass a class, that's all he or she usually accomplishes. But when a student is motivated to learn a particular subject—and sets goals for himself—higher grades and even more importantly, much more knowledge always follow.

Set your sights high! With God's help you can accomplish the goals and desires of your heart.

The Joy of Work

Life is even more wonderful when we find joy in our tasks and happiness in little things—like getting organized. Go through your school papers. Throw out what you don't need, file what you do need, and find a place to store things. You might want to run to an office supply store for some storage boxes, or you can use whatever is around the house. Be creative! Make your storage arrangements tidy and attractive.

Somehow I can't **believe** that there are any heights that can't be scaled by a man who knows **the secrets** of making dreams come true. This special secret, it seems to me, can be summarized in four C's. They are **curiosity, confidence**, courage, and constancy, and the greatest of all is confidence. When you believe in a thing, **believe in** it all the way, implicitly and unquestionably.

WALT DISNEY

Dreams

Hold fast to dreams
For if dreams die
Life is a broken-winged bird
That cannot fly.

Hold fast to dreams
For when dreams go
Life is a barren field
Frozen with snow.

LANGSTON HUGHES

Heavenly Father,

There is so much I want to accomplish today. You know my dreams and goals. You know I'm a little scared about taking a few steps forward toward those dreams. Please be with me today, Father.

Thank you, O God, for those dreams and goals that you have planted in my heart—and for giving me the wisdom to know which ones matter most. Help me to pursue them with your strength and direction.

But even more importantly, Father, help me to always press toward the greatest goal and greatest prize of all—to love you with all my heart. When I get caught up in my own plans, remind me through the Holy Spirit that the greatest prize of all is knowing you!

Every good and perfect gift is from above, coming down from the Father of the heavenly lights, who does not change like shifting shadows.

JAMES 1:17

True contentment is the power of getting of any situation all that there is in it.

G. K. CHESTERTON

WHAT A WONDERFUL GIFT

WHAT AN INCREDIBLE TIME IN YOUR LIFE THIS IS! SAVOR
THIS CHANCE TO CELEBRATE YOUR ACCOMPLISHMENTS,
OPPORTUNITIES, FRIENDS, AND FAMILY.

If you **think** **education** is expensive, try **ignorance.**

DEREK BOK

SCHOOL DAZE

Before you complain too much about the amount of time you spent in school (for most students in America, about 164 days a year)—and you wouldn't complain, would you?—consider the countries that have the highest number of mandatory school days!

China	251
Japan	243
Korea	220
Israel	215
Germany	210
Russia	210
Switzerland	207
Netherlands	200

Yes, it's wonderful to be blessed with the gift of an education—and sometimes it's wonderful to get an all-day recess!

A Book Look

Charlie "Tremendous" Jones says you will be the same person in five years that you are today except for two things: the people with whom you associate and the books you read.

Though you've done your share of reading during school, your reading career has just begun! Just think how much you can benefit from reading—

- Just as physical exercise makes you stronger, reading makes you mentally sharper.
- As you read about important subjects, you broaden your understanding and grow intellectually.
- When you read, you learn to communicate better and have more interesting things to say.

- Ever since Gutenberg invented the printing press to mass produce the Bible, the printed word has been linked with spiritual growth.

The most important thing you can read, of course, is God's Word. What a great way to start and end your day! Peter tells us to "always be prepared to give an answer to everyone who asks you to give the reason for the hope that you have" (1 Peter 3:15).

Take advantage of all the reading opportunities around you; as a result, you'll grow mentally and spiritually and make your life more wonderful.

I delight in your decrees;
I will not neglect your word.

PSALM 119:16

God's **gifts**
put man's
best dreams
to shame.

ELIZABETH BARRETT BROWNING

On May 29, 1953, Edmund Hillary and Tenzing Norgay reached the summit of Mount Everest—the first human beings ever to do so. That day, they became heroes, icons of achievement in a still war-weary world. Hillary said of their accomplishment, "It is not the mountain we conquer but ourselves."

Today is an important day in your life story—today you get to choose which mountains you'll climb, which goals you'll set for yourself, and how you'll go about fulfilling them. Who knows what great challenges and tasks God will set before you?

Remember that he goes with you, and will use you in amazing ways.

For nothing is impossible with God.

LUKE 1:37

We were filled with laughter, and we sang for joy. And the other nations said, "What amazing things the Lord has done for them." Yes, the Lord has done amazing things for us! What joy!

PSALM 126:2, 3 NLT

If you have lived, take thankfully the past.

JOHN DRYDEN

Remember

What do you have to be thankful for?
Right now, make a list of the ways
you've been blessed—think of your
education and school opportunities,
your family and friends, all the
fun you've had over the years.
Take some time to write a few special
thank-you notes to parents, siblings,
friends, or teachers who have been an
encouragement and blessing to you.
They'll be blessed by your gratitude—
and so will you!

There is not a more **pleasing** exercise of the mind than gratitude. It is accompanied with such an inward **satisfaction** that the duty is sufficiently **rewarded** by the performance.

JOSEPH ADDISON

69

When I was a boy of fourteen, my father was so ignorant I could hardly stand to have the old man around. But when I got to be twenty-one, I was astonished at how much he had learned in seven years.

MARK TWAIN

Listen to your father, who gave you life, and don't despise your mother's experience when she is old.

PROVERBS 23:22 NLT

Honor Your Parents!

Graduation is one of those key moments in life that marks new beginnings. Even if you are not yet ready to move from home, your relationship with your parents will undergo changes.

A few things that shouldn't change, however, include—

- A sense of appreciation for all they have done for you
- A spirit of respect and love toward them
- A desire to maintain a relationship with them even as you embark on a new journey of life

One of the Ten Commandments is to honor our parents (Exodus 20:12). And what makes that Commandment different than all the others is that God ties a promise to it. If we honor our parents, our reward is a long and fruitful life. Loving your parents helps make your life wonderful!

Thank You, God...

For friends who make me laugh
For a family that loves me
For teachers who challenge me to grow
For a coach who makes me work
For opportunities to help others
For a preacher who proclaims truth
For the person who helped me
    turn my life around
For the grace and power to forgive
    those who have hurt me
For someone who is praying for me
For your forgiveness.

Dear Heavenly Father,

Thanks for this time in my life.
God, I have all kinds of parties and
ceremonies coming up—help me relish
every moment of the coming weeks
and give you thanks for everything
you've helped me accomplish.

God, give me the words to encourage
my friends and thank my family.

Most of all, thank you for being
with me and helping me reach
this point. Thank you so much
for your presence in my life.

"For I know the plans I have for you," declares the Lord, "plans to prosper you and not to harm you, plans to give you hope and a future."

JEREMIAH 29:11

Faith makes the uplook good, the outlook bright, the inlook favorable, and the future glorious.

V. RAYMOND EDMAN

WHAT A WONDERFUL FUTURE

LIFE IS WONDERFUL TODAY BECAUSE WE ALSO HAVE
THE HOPE OF WONDERFUL TOMORROWS. WHO KNOWS
WHAT WONDERFUL THINGS GOD HAS IN STORE FOR YOU?

Great
opportunities
to help others
seldom come,
but **small ones**
surround
us daily.

SALLY KOCH

Where Is Your Calcutta?

Mother Teresa has inspired millions of people with her life of sacrificial service. One such woman was so affected by her life and calling that she decided to give up her privileged life in the United States, move to Calcutta, and share in Mother Teresa's ministry.

When Mother Teresa heard of the woman's plans, she did not respond with the expected enthusiasm. Instead, she wrote the woman this brief, yet profound, reply: "Find your own Calcutta."

Where is your Calcutta? Perhaps it's right in your own back yard.

What matters most to me is to finish what God started: the job the Master Jesus gave me of letting everyone I meet know all about this incredibly extravagant generosity of God.

ACTS 20:24 THE MESSAGE

When Trouble Comes

Dear brothers and sisters, whenever trouble comes your way, let it be an opportunity for joy. For when your faith is tested, your endurance has a chance to grow. So let it grow, for when your endurance is fully developed, you will be strong in character and ready for anything.

JAMES 1:2-4 NLT

Do not **pray** for easy lives, pray to be **stronger men**. Do not pray for tasks equal to your powers, but for powers equal to your tasks.

PHILLIPS BROOKS

A Wonderful Goal

People who articulate their dreams, goals, and plans tend to be more successful at achieving desired results and feeling a sense of purpose. What are some of the dreams and goals you have for your life? Write down four or five major goals for your life. List one that could be accomplished in the next year and another that could take several years to realize. Under each goal, write down three or four specific action steps.

Good plans shape good decisions. That's why good planning helps to make the elusive dreams come true.

LESTER R. BITTEL

Let us throw off everything that hinders and the sin that so easily entangles, and let us run with perseverance the race marked out for us.

HEBREWS 12:1

Heavenly Father,

Sometimes I get scared
about the future. Please help me
remember that you have taken care
of me every step of the way,
and that you have amazing
plans for my life.

God,
What I want for my life
is to follow you, and I know that
as I do, you'll make life amazing.
Thank you for your love.

Give thanks to the Lord, for he is good; his love endures forever.

PSALM 107:1

God designed the human machine to run on Himself. He Himself is the fuel our spirits were designed to burn, or the food our spirits were designed to feed on. There is no other.

C.S. LEWIS

WHAT A WONDERFUL GOD

The real reason that life is wonderful is because that's the way God created it to be. Your life is richer when you say thanks to the giver of all good gifts.

If the blind
put their hand
in God's, they find
their way more surely
than those who see
but have not faith
or purpose.

HELEN KELLER

GOD IS SO WONDERFUL THAT HE ...

Created a marvelous world for us to live in (see Genesis 1:1)

Knew us and loved us before we were even born
(see Psalm 139:13-16)

Gives us fresh mercies every single morning (see Lamentations 3:25)

Meets our every need (see Philippians 4:19)

Helps us when times are tough (see Psalm 46:1)

Forgives us from our sins (see 1 John 1:9)

Promises to give us peace (see John 14:27)

Lives in our hearts (see Revelation 3:20)

Helps us overcome our fears (see Psalm 56:11)

Protects us from evil (see 2 Thessalonians 3:3)

Gives us confidence (see Philippians 4:13)

Guides our paths (see Psalm 32:8)

Comforts us when we are sad—and helps
us comfort others (see 2 Corinthians. 1:3-4)

Grants us eternal life (see John 10:27-28)

Be sure to fear the Lord and sincerely worship him.
Think of all the wonderful things he has done for you.

2 CORINTHIANS 9:15, NLT

Amazing grace!
How sweet the sound
That **saved a wretch**
like me! I once was
lost, but now am
found; **Was blind,**
but now I see.

JOHN NEWTON

Amazing Grace

Most people have heard the song "Amazing Grace," but few know the story behind the song and its writer.

Born in 1725, John Newton followed his father, the commander of a merchant ship, into a life on the sea. Through some skill and much brutality, John worked his way to captain on a ship in the slave trade. But on May 10, 1748, in the midst of a raging storm, the previously non-religious Newton cried out to God, "Save us." And God did.

Humbled by such mercy, Newton left the slave trade, became a minister, and became one of the great voices in England speaking out against buying and selling humans.

God's amazing grace can change even the most wretched of lives and create a new wonderful, person.

Therefore, if anyone is in Christ, he is a new creation; the old has gone, the new has come!

2 CORINTHIANS 5:17

The Clock Maker

An old-fashioned mechanical wind-up alarm clock contains about a dozen moving parts. If that kind of clock washed up on the beach, no one would dare suggest that this simple machine came together by chance. An intelligent designer and skilled worker were needed to put it together.

And yet there are still a few who argue that a planet containing 9,000 species of birds, 70,000 kinds of trees, and 750,000—and counting—types of insects does not require an intelligent maker to exist.

We do live in a wonderful world, which is the gift of a wonderful creator!

Christ is the one through whom God created everything in heaven and earth. He made the things we can see and the things we can't see— kings, kingdoms, rulers, and authorities. Everything has been created through him and for him.

COLOSSIANS 1:16 NLT

Choose This Day

Many graduates get thrown into a busy post-graduation life and have trouble continuing a habit of prayer and church attendance. On a note card, write a one- or two-sentence commitment to yourself to worship regularly, both in church and individually. Below that, list a few ways to make good on that commitment: keep Sunday mornings free from work, go to bed by midnight on Saturday nights, get up early enough for time to read scripture, pray, and listen to worship music. Sign your card and put it somewhere you'll see it often—in your Bible or on your desk.

So then, just as you received Christ Jesus as Lord, continue to live in him, rooted and built up in him, strengthened in the faith as you were taught, and overflowing with thankfulness.

COLOSSIANS 2:6, 7

93

Never be afraid to trust an unknown future to a known God.

CORRIE TEN BOOM

Father,

I remember today how wonderful you really are. You have saved me. You have brought amazing blessings my way. And I know you have a bright future in store for me.

God, I choose to thank you and trust you even when things get stormy. Thank you for your goodness to me.

Heavenly Father,

Thank you for creating a world
filled with wonder and delight. Thank you
for family and friends that make my life
so rich. Thank you that you want me to find
pleasure in following your will and ways.

God,

I know that you are good. Help me
remember that my life is in your hands.

I am so thankful and blessed to join
the celebration you have created
for our enjoyment.

Amen.